Do you dream in colour

By

W. B. Allison

"I love you" she said,
"I love you but I'm still leaving".

Introduction and notes from the author

This books opens up on two short stories 'The symphony', written in 2021, which follows a nameless young man who while exploring finds himself confronting a very unfamiliar and unusual circumstance, the story follows his perspective and his experiences set within the modern age, following that is a story called 'The lady of lake Charlatan', 2022, a piece not unlike folklore of the past this one begins with the protagonist whom finds himself met by a mysterious woman sailing in the lake, the story follows their meet, their eventual falling for each other, but later discovering that there may be a permissive sense of evil intention.

Neither is based on real events, even if some of the views or traits of the characters may be based on real people, this is not an allegorical story and was written for creative pleasures primarily.

In addition, there are dozens of poems and sonnets written from 2020-2022, that are placed afterwards to be read and enjoyed as separate pieces of material to the other stories. Poems including 'Rising waters', 'World appeal', and 'The stranger at your door'.

The author is quoted as saying "part IIII demonstrated an enormous shift in the quality of my written work, I can tell a big difference between the rest of this book and that part, even if the other poetry was only written shortly before, what part IIII consists of, is by far my finest work yet".

Part I

But for you the sky shall never go black,
The sun will smile at you and you'll smile
back.

The symphony

The unkept naturally placed blades of grass twisted around the feet of any who would walk through the pathway into the woods, they grew so tall along with the dozens of flowers that made up the spaces between the trees, so many different species all bunched together, it would be impossible to grab a handful at random and have only one kind in your palm when you looked back.

Although dwarfed by the greatly impressive tree trunks that penetrated the ground, as if they could not be separated from where they stood, with roots that went as deep as hell itself, and scattered at the foot of the trees grew wild mushrooms. The trees were brown in colour, texture, and character, they stood like soldiers ordered to guard nothing but each other, all standing there, alike and yet unlike.

A young man, as described by anyone older than he, waltzed aimlessly deeper, the sounds of the natural world increased, with birds singing scripted symphonies as if it were for his ears only, like a personal fanfare, coupled with the howling of the wind smacking the trees, plucking, and then cascading the leaves all around, dropping down but then shooting upwards as if they were ascending to the heavens.

The sun's rays that punctured through the breaks in the branches, would illuminate the grass lands, like a spotlight shining on this orchestra of sound, and as they drove towards a crescendo, the rain began to pour like it was the grand finale.

The rain was heavy, and the peaceful sounds of the birds began to diminish, water would run down the body of the trees and mix into the saps that spilled. A more fanciful person than he would say the trees cried their orange tears, weeping for the insects that were dying from the plague of the sky, he thought to himself, something insignificant to us is not so much to them, as the rain danced over his face.

But as he walked deeper into the woods, the natural protection that the many overlapping branches provided, was now working against him, as they filed the rainwater in large quantities towards him, showering his head, looking for cover he came to a small wall made of jagged rock, it came no more than three feet from the ground and so would not provide much shield from the rain.

On the other side of the wall was a small wooden raft floating in the river, tied to bamboo poles stuck into the ground, the raft was no bigger than the front door of his house, though much more aged than it, the raft by the looks of it was older than the young man was himself, it was made of a combination of withered wooden beams and ropes to tie it all together.

Lazily drifting back and forth in the river this small raft, that he named the Huckleberry ferry, kept pushing up against the jagged wall, as well as hitting some of the rocks that were on the riverbed, no doubt why it was coming apart at the corners he thought, and so he wondered who built it and how long it had been there for, it would have been built to pass over the river to the other side where there was a woods much like the one he was in, though to him the two didn't look to be part of one large forest.

Hoping for shelter though he followed the wall line it led him to a small, darkened cave-like area. His longed curled hair dripping wet, as much as his clothes did, he sat on a rounded stone and waited out the rain. Taking off his boots along with his socks and leaving them to dry beside him, unsure of how long had past, though he thought it could not be more than an hour he wondered when the rain would stop, boring himself in his own head, he started to write in the book he always carried with him, he was a great fan of poetry and so kept it with him for whenever he gets a seed of inspiration, he would often write it down so he would remember it.

Flicking through the pages to where he penned his latest work, and rereading some of his work he had planned for an anthology book, he came to the most recent poem he had written, though he had not decided if it was finished yet, thinking to speak it out loud would give him his answer, he sat as comfortably as he could on the grey stone and recited his poem thus far:

Once free souls brought low,
with identical uniforms they know better than their own skin,
nothing but the sound of the machine filling their ears,
like the whistle of a kettle with their hearts ready to boil over,
spilling onto the surface of the dead-end life they live,
how did it come to this?

Just the words hitting the air as his tongue slapped the back of his teeth, trying to get his mouth moving to deliver the lines well, he felt within himself that it was good enough to finish there. Thinking to himself, the young man pondered on what the words would mean to other people when they read it, will they know what it is about, or will they invent new meanings that are applicable only to them. As his father thinks that the poem is about war when he intended to write as someone else writing about their job.

He had thought of the idea to switch the perspective from first person, that he usually wrote in, to third, and so imagined himself as someone else writing about their job and how they feel about it, for experimental reasons if not for anything else, as all writers need to find out who they are within the words they deliver.

Although still he recognised a soldier is a job and he understood how someone could think it was about war, after he mentioned about uniform and a sense of duty. He often remarked that the great thing about art is that it is subjective and an incredibly personal media, all opinions on a piece are valid to each other. He went on to say, in his own head, even if it is a fictional comment on working, it makes him appear to be more of a serious writer to himself and hopefully to others if he says he is writing about war, as war throughout history has been a muse of artists but at the same time, has always been taken seriously as a subject. Lifting his head from his book, with the crack of his neck and the clearing of his throat, he could still hear the rain hitting the ground, a moment of thought lingered on the bird song he heard before, as he wondered around the darker crevasses of the cave, he found himself in, and just as he turned back to where he was sitting a voice from the dark made itself known to him. And he stopped frozen in body and time.

The lady of lake charlatan

Waterlilies sway on the lake of glitter and mud,
Pale birds sing stories of what they've seen before,
The sedge grows in parties along the grounded flood,
And the flowers be all of dreary stem and petals torn.

A wooden craft sets upon the water sighted still,
A woman of youthful beauty, skin fair and hair of golden
bled,
 Lulling to herself to warden off the winter chill,
Cloaked in linen sheets of purple and red.

"Where go you?" I begged, as her neck turned and her eyes
met me,
Voice of titillating nature she beckoned with her song,
She was courteous and receptive to my courtesies it
seems,
Filled with effervescence, her speech carried for long.

The morrows hours grew long and her song not yet
undone,
I sat upon her boat, both hungry eyed and head a fever
dream of spring,
She did sing to me with fingers pressed upon a carved
green stone,
As we sailed on the river, words of love was all I could only
come to string.

"I beg to those who above me rule and control what I
endure and what I face,

Whichever force it is that steers my course, directs my
soul and guides thou,
May you wash ones own into the reaches of her embrace,
May you abstain my sin, relinquish my trespasses and let
us together be for now".

I said this without a care as if some sort of opioid dream I
hath become,
Knowing all along, in my head it was unlike my normal
speech,
But to my heart outpoured reasoning, internal
overpowering it had done,
And so I gave in to my good hearts oppressive reach.

She cried aloud, "I will be deaf to prayerful minds that
intrude on expressive turns,
Hence from the mind of simpletons, simple ideas only do
come forthwith,
Speak to me of love, and love by thine own words is what
shall be earned,
Say not words filled abundant with gods, angels and
myth."

A stroke of blessings do set themselves on my heart,
And so to, she took me to sit under the protection of the
willow tree,
Her thighs cleft, and in turn brings them only under
themselves to be apart,
I gave my divine love to thee.

She spoke in words that formed clearly when thou
reached my ears,
"If you leave me so, you do me wrong", she said as she
stared into me with eyes blue,

And so I spoke the words, before I thought them, the ones
she was anxious to hear,
I replied "What fortune I have found, no need to feel
worried are you".

A twisted smile brought upon her face and fire hath
become her eyes in haste,
Her arms on my shoulder came forth for me to steady,
And here I do lie, with no time to me hath been seemingly
waste,
She laughed and said, "I aimed so near in my assumptions
already".

I slipped into slumber thereafter with her song poured
into my ears,
"Withdraw your words or repent for the causality of such"
Birds and demons alike spoke these words to me in my
dream and confirmed in fear,
I have strayed into the waters for too long and sank myself
too much.

Voice trembling I said, "Thou shall not stir ones foot to
seek redemption, speak in unattained words"
I demanded from them to tell me what they knew,
Sense drained from my being, and the vain voices was all
that was to be heard,
I was left by her, defenceless and turned
axis askew.

I awoke and spoke outwards in a cry "if you leave me so,
you do me wrong,
Honourable reckoning are you not, I see what it is you
hide",

My eyes were once shrouded in red cloth, now comes the end of her siren song,
My foolishness hath become me, as I remain all alone here by the cold lake side.

Part II

Do you really think they'll drop the bombs?

Generational lifestyle

(The happy sad moments)

Stolen moments of freedom in hotel rooms,
With random people and friends alike,
Breaking off for a few minutes talking to the moon,
Sat up there in the dark sky of midnight.

Do everything you can to relinquish the hurt,
Widened pupils, coming up only to fall,
Blood turning to alcohol spilling on your best shirt,
Sex with strangers, then only missed calls.

That was then....

As it sets, we kiss the sun goodbye,
And watch as it drifts down the falling sky,
And catch the wind from the summer breeze.

Still you're so much kinder on the eyes,
As we sit in comfort on cloud nine,
Now I'm exactly where I'm meant to be.

Your skins pale, white from the twilight sky,
After the moon illuminates your best side,
And that is all I really need.

We're two souls of a different kind,
And I'll ride the helter skelter of your mind,
And you know exactly what I mean.

.... And this is now

Say the same things that we said before,
Cause we both know we should have talked much more,
But that was then and this is now.

I always tried to say what I meant,
And so I wish this isn't how it had to end,
But how to fix this, we don't know how.

We hide behind words we know are lies,
Because it makes it easier to say goodbye,
Now too much was said to try and work it out.

As the sun set, it set on us too,
And now I can't help but have hate for you,
I'm not even sure what this fight is about.

Clinging too tight

I'm tired now of you living under my skin,
Talking in my ear and watching my every step,
Because it's making my resilience wear too thin,
So now I'm afraid this is what you must accept,
You have to stop sitting in my shadow,
You pressure me by putting all your faith in me,
Like I'd be able to take away your sorrow,
But you must understand that this not who I had planned
to be.

Pink gin and lemonade

And I can't help that I think of you,
When the place I found my drink was you,
And so you're always on my mind,
Every time I order mine,
So what am I now to do.

Things always move too fast

I guess we ran out of time,
Because soon enough, the sand passes through the hour
glass.

So what are we now,
I couldn't hold onto you, and things they always seem to
move too fast.

But I'm not on top of the world,
Even now you're gone, you still have a hold over me.

Although I have someone else,
They still can't, hold a candle to what you had been.

And I know it's a selfish thing,
To keep her on my line, even when I still say your name.

But what am I to do,
Now looking back, I can never again be the same.

Hard fought

I only realised I wasted my time once the sand had ran out,
And I found what I was looking for, but you said you've
had enough,
Telling me how I blew my last chance, once again,
Even though now I'm trying to get it back to the good
times we had.

So don't throw it all away, like our love wasn't hard fought.

Those in between nights

With my rose tinted eyes that see only the best in you,
You blow through the good times in my mind,
And I hate that you only call me by my name now,
But its on the nights we don't do much talking of any kind.

I know what I said, but it's not what I meant,
And now you give me too many reasons not to go home,
I want the company that I had I taken for granted before,
As now I sink in waves of nostalgia that hit when I'm
alone.

I am within and yet still I am without,
As my heart and my hands work overtime on you,
Perplexing thoughts of love and lust consume me,
And I've come to see you know not what it is that you do.

Breakup goggles

Under the halo of the twilight moon,
That shines above me, sitting in the night sky,
I drift alone on cobble stone streets,
With my memories triggered as I walk on by.

I keep thinking on the days,
When your words were getting under my skin,
I keep trying to block it out from my brain,
But you always find your way in.

Thinking on it often makes me wonder,
Why it still feels better being with you than without,
And so sometimes I can't help but ponder,
If all I should have done in the first place was hear you out.

Street of dreams

I live on the street of dreams,
Reality always seemed a little too harsh for me,
It doesn't mean I'm out of touch with the way the world is,
I just choose to live in an internally nicer place.

No one prepares you for the death of your parents

One day you'll have to be the shoulder for your mother to
cry on,
But then who's shoulder will there be left for you once
she's gone,
And once she's gone you will feel like there is no where
you can belong,
But someday you will, like we all are, be told to move on.

All over again

I know you're not just a lover but my best friend,
From the way you look at me with deep devotion,
It makes me want to fall in love with you all over again,
And forever feel this euphoric emotion.

The great days still coming

It's strange that the bad times make you realise the good ones,
And you never noticed the good days while it was happening,
You were living the best days waiting for better ones that never came,
And now you only wish you could go back and do it again.

But life doesn't work out like that, and it never did,
So what can you do now but be thankful for the good days you had,
And the great days you still have coming up,
They'll be great this time because you won't take them for granted again.

Clay kicker

Do you know what it's like to dig your own grave,
When each breath you take means you're stealing air from the man beside you,
Another tunnel collapses but the people above the ground are saved,
Clawing for air as the churned high ground starts to break through.

The love that fell to the seabed

I'm just as content as you to let the storms rage,
And as for reconciliation, I'd rather die under the waves,
They say you either rise above it or it consumes you,
But now I don't have a care of what it is that you do.

The prideful hate that you have in your heart is evident,
And for your place in my heart, you'll die of irrelevance.

The end of time

I can understand I have nothing in sight,
For now it's only the stars that shine,
Yet in my heart I have no form of plight,
So long as I can still drink my wine.

Your life is fleeting the same as mine,
And after it your death lasts till end of time.

Best part of us

Love is the best thing that we can give someone,
A piece of ourselves that is most precious,
Although it's undefinable to say where it comes from,
It is still known to be the best part of us.

Flaky morality

Skin flaking like breadcrumbs of a stale biscuit,
Tears streaming as if all I do is cry,
And within your lies I was made complicit,
Now the trust in our relationship walks out to die.

He told me to hang you

I asked god,
But he told me to hang you.

Like a metal rod,
You were cold through and through.

Cause from the start,
You showed me nothing but indifferent.

Now within my heart,
I have been made belligerent.

You can give your all

You can give your life to the company,
Only to be replaced come Monday morning.

You can give your love to somebody,
Only for them to take back all they said to you.

You can give your energy to help a friend,
Only for them to turn their back when you need them
most.

You can give your time to your children,
Only for them to never call you when they're grown.

You can give your all, at any moment,
And never get back that which you had given.

Value

We all wish that we could live forever,
We all try to do something of value,
Striving hard no matter the endeavour,
To leave something behind, greater than you.

The small moments

For the everyday person life has few great moments,
So we must focus on the simple pleasures,
The air in the forest,
A new tube of tooth paste,
Holding hands with your lover,
Talking to your grandparents,
Days when you don't have to wear socks,
Eating a meal with your family,
Hearing a song you use to love,
When you make someone smile,
Finishing a book,
Marking days off until Christmas,
A drink with ice cubes in,
Buying a candle,
'Just because' flowers,
Seeing an old friend,
Fresh bedding,
The sound of rain,
Watching tv with your parents,
Sleeping until the afternoon,
A call from your brother just to check in,
Or writing a poem.

Footprints

There are footprints on the beach,
They're a perfect match to the size of mine,
But they're laid out ahead of me,
Stretching out as I walk in their place.

The waves wash out what has already been,
And what is left are only small imprints,
Like memory fragments from the passing of time,
They're always changing slightly each time a new wave
comes in.

I can see the beach around me,
But there is neither sun, nor rain, nor any noticeable
weather,
Just the face of God, a white clouded sky that reaches far
above me,
Giving of light, but it has no form or significant.

But for the fact it makes me wonder what is beyond the
beach,
I can't tell where I am or where I'm on my way to,
I just keep walking further and further,
And what I fear most, is the day I catch up to the footprints
ahead of me.

A hero's death

A coward dies many times before his death,
But a brave man lives on even past his,
Through the memory of his act,
Through the inspiration he created,
He lives forever in stories and in the hearts of the people.

Never feeling comfortable again

The times are getting harder as my days are getting
shorter,
And recently my life isn't easy,
And so what if I want to stay home today,
Does that make me lazy.

Is there a god?

I understand only what I hold in my hand,
And if I can't feel it, I don't believe.

God holds no place unless I can see it's face,
And if I can't see it, I don't believe.

No one should ever be forgotten

The hardest truths are often too heavy to speak out load,
There is great emotion that stands behind the words felt,
Words that are so much a part of the human heart,
They are the words of memory, that one should ever be
forgotten.

My way back

The only thing I saw on my walk down memory lane,
Is that I couldn't find my way back,
And the only thing I found, on my way back around,
Is that I was always on the wrong track.

Us breaking up caused me nothing but pain,
And now it's all I can feel inside,
So what can I do, now that I'm without you,
I am a byproduct of a lack of pride.

How long does a heart stay broken for

How many words does it take to tear a life apart,
How many sleepless nights does it take to fix a broken
heart,
And how many times will you walk at night alone through
the park,
And all you're wondering is how many years will it take to
get back to the start.

No better feeling

There is no better moment than waking up to the one you love,
No better taste than theirs on your lips,
No better sight than their smile when they're happy,
And no better sound than the first time they tell you they love you.

There is no better feeling than the feeling of love.

A shooting star

I saw the radiance of a beam of light,
So pure in it's form that it split the sky,
It raced across the darkened night,
So beautiful to me it made me cry,
With tear filled eyes that engulfed my sight,
I watched with wonder as it passed me by.

Inside we're all the same

I want to go outside and not hide away,
I want to sleep all night to see a better day,
I want to forget all the words I had to say,
I want to be myself and hope and pray,
That someday I won't be afraid,
Of who I am and come what may,
You and I, we will be able to play,
With whoever no matter how they're made,
And we won't ever have to play this game,
Cause inside we are all just the same.

Empty frames

The bedroom that sleeps no one,
After you woke up for the last time,
Cherished pictures hung high on the walls,
But now there is nothing but sorrow solidified.

The air is thinner than it use to be,
The pain from your passing clouds the room,
Not even is there the sight of the sun,
Or the scent of your inescapable perfume.

Important letters and spam thrown away,
The sound of a pair of earrings hits the floor,
Gold, silver and diamond taken alike,
But some of the people have never been here before.

You ran out of days you would have wasted,
Dust collected on books never read,
The room is bereft of all your collections,
Nothing but empty frames above the bed.

We march

We march,
For our families,
For our country,
We march.

We march,
For our possessions,
For our friends,
We march.

We march,
For our lives,
For our children,
We march.

We march,
For our freedom,
Against oppression,
We march.

We march,
For each other,
Side by side with brothers,
We march.

Finally

And the flower that grows upon the grave of our
relationship,
Shall be there as a reminder for what is gone,
A memory it is now, and so in the past it shall sit,
Which confirms in our minds, that to thrive is to move on.

Love was not enough to save us from each other,
And now I can only make peace with our current state,
I still remain we were necessary for the growth of one
another
And I understand it all now finally, but finally was too late.

When you were mine

I'd gladly waste my life away,
By sitting in the sunshine all day,
Never seeing the night sky,
And you and I will never die,
Cause only in the sunshine,
Is when you were still mine.

Keep going

Somedays you may feel yourself beat,
And you feel you may never again see the sun,
And somedays you may feel nothing but defeat,
And you'll wonder what it was you have done.

But just keep on keeping on.

Because soon you'll see that it's not going to last,
When all of the clear waters will be a revival,
All of the aggravations will be of the past,
And you'll thrive with the ultimate survival.

They do say

They do say, that we should never talk out loud the secrets
we keep inside,
But then you hear, "if you trust me with yours, I can trust
you with mine".

They do say, about the dreams we have put on hold,
That you better try for those dreams cause soon you'll be
too old.

They do say, that you have to earn a living,
And after that you'll get back all you had given.

And then they say, to enjoy life while it's still yours,
Cause soon your days speed up and then there will
eventually be no more.

Vacation

Waiting at the station,
Ready for a vacation,
From the rain.

I finally got the option,
Not to be stuck in my situation,
Once again.

Raindrops

Day 1:
I spent my entire day in bed,
With raindrops falling on my head,
Through the cracks that form they drip in my ear,
And they block out the noise so they're all I can hear,
Once more I spent my entire day in bed.

Day 14:
I spent my entire day in bed,
I'm now drowning to the depths inside my own head,
So many overwhelming troubles but I let it fill,
And I keep remaining here, laying perfectly still,
Once more I spent my entire day in bed.

No one should ever be forgotten
(Version 2)

Keep with you the important things and hold them dear,
I was scared to go through life and no one ever notice I
was here,
So the best thing to do is to leave some words behind to
put in your stead,
Cause it's a terrifying thought that most people are
forgotten after they're dead.

Carry that weight

When someone dies there's a temptation never to talk
about them again,
As a fear the pain will come back,
But in order to keep, those who are now gone,
You must carry that weight with you.

?

What's the difference,
Between living
And waiting to die?

Looking back

Don't waste your time looking back,
You're not going that way,
Surge forward on your own track,
And say only what you mean to say.

Grey clouds are falling on your head

Sometimes in life you just need to be sad,
And you know it's okay to feel that way,
It may remind you of what you once had,
But I hope those grey clouds pass on some day.

Overthinking

Do you have those nights when you're in too deep,
Drowning in your head,
Wide awake in your bed,
And there's no remedy to help you sleep.

You either

You either kiss me or blacken my eye,
You either love me or leave me to die,
I either laugh or I break down and cry,
While you break my heart and I wonder why.

A great amount of nothing

You're told "these are the best days of your life",
If that's the case I feel I was cheated,
"You need to get yourself a husband or a wife",
As this life is not something to be repeated.

Life seems just a story with no meaning,
And with my life I always thought there would be more,
At the end i amassed a great amount of nothing,
Because I still know not what it is we live for.

Be

Be yourself, always walk with who you are,
Be okay, with where you're at no matter where it is,
Be happy, with the people who you're with,
And always be kind, to those who you meet.

The smell of the battle field

Endless noise and the smoke turns the sky black,
The slaughter ensures that the front and the rear man
dies,
No one is clean but the leaders at the back,
And so we will all be buried together side by side,
But it will not be in any grave our families can see,
The piles of bodies overlap telling nothing to no one,
Our lives were thrown out like they were free,
So much death it's hard to say if either side won.

Tongue tied

Your ears are cheated from the things you heard,
Who you have become is not who you planned,
A tongue tied world breads a battle of words,
And it's clear, most of don't understand.

How it's going

Trying to piece myself back together,
But you insist on tearing me apart,
I have not known hate for any other,
And yet I still love you with all my heart.

Comfortable silence

We say I love you just to pass the time now,
As we sit in the silence that we made comfortably,
But the love left our hearts so long ago it means nothing,
Only words, cause now we've ran out of things we can say.

Part lll

*Cause now your
'over the rainbow'.*

*Has turned to
bars in your window.*

She said

Physically close but it's like a lifetime of emotions apart,
Saying I love you feels tainted, black and sour in my mouth,
It now feels more like the end rather than the start,
With problems that have risen from within as well as without.

I'm worried that even this is better than living a life alone,
While the look on her face says all the words i needed to know,
It's a strange distance that forms and makes it's presence known,
A break up's own version of a closing ceremony show.

And in her eyes theres definitely not love, but nor is it hate,
There's a silence that's formed that to me seems obscured,
It's just emptiness, like a washed of hands oriented state,
And now I can see the words that don't need to be heard.

It struck my heart like a lightning bolt when she said,
The love she once had for me was now dead.

Icarus (said 3 times)

What would it be like to learn how to fly,
What is it you see when you look up at the sky,
Burnt out is that poor old Icarus,
But now he doesn't even take the time to look at us,
From the greatest of heights come the biggest fall,
And now he wishes he'd never even tried at all.

A leech named Lucy

If I said no you'd say yeah,
You made me swear and swear,
You trying dulling my brain,
Made us think the same.

With red flags everywhere,
But maybe I didn't care,
Or maybe I was just blind,
Cause you had broken my mind.

You suck my blood like a leech,
You brought me down to my knees,
Always spoke out of turn,
Your actions showed me new hurt.

You ripped my body apart,
Tore my soul from my the heart,
Till i was lifeless and pale,
I was tasteless and stale.

You hid your intentions so well,
It seemed like no one could tell,
What your pain put me through,
Cause they still all love you.

You cut the lines for the phone,
Always kept me at home,
I couldn't go outside,
You'd make me cower and hide.

I just cried and cried,
And now I wish I had died,

But now I need you to know,
I just can't take anymore.

I would always let you,
Do the things that you do,
But you would never let me,
And now I can see.

You were no good for me,
Cut my skin till it bleeds,
My bodies black and blue,
Cause of the things that you do.

You said no one would believe me,
That I'm just a man,
how could I be the victim here,
You're a leach,
Named Lucy,
And I wish I'd never met you.

You gave the impression you cared,
I would have taken you there,
Or taken you at your word,
Now it seems so absurd.

You command and you preach,
Make my decisions for me,
I felt I had no voice,
I couldn't stop all the noise.

I cut off family and friends,
You said it was us to the end,
You kept me locked in a cage,
Filled with turmoil and rage.

How could you do this to me,
You make me beg on my knees,
For what it rightfully mine,
I got out just in time.

You took my joy and my smile,
But you did it with such style,
So that I couldn't tell,
You put me through hell.

I think it was June the first,
When it got to it's worst,
You nearly took my life,
I still remember that night.

When I forgot my own name,
While you just played your game,
But I always was true,
You know I did still love you.

You left a man in my bed,
You wanted him instead,
And now I feel like a fool,
For ever loving you.

For you I gave up my pride,
I plucked the stars from the sky,
For you so you could be mine,
But I feel I wasted my time.

You're a leech named Lucy,
And I wish Id never met you.

Who do you want to be?

Do you feel you got everything,
Brought everything you wanted to bring,
The dreams you had when you were young,
The song that you ending leaving unsung.

Or all those songs you wrote about,
When you felt within and you felt without,
Who is it you want to be,
Who is it you want them to see.

What if I just won't be,
Who I thought I was going to be,
What if I will never achieve,
All the things I once had dreamed.

Or maybe you will never go,
To all the places you want to go,
Cause now your body is getting slow,
And there's no time left anymore.

I think we can still just pretend,
That this isn't where it's gunna end,
We made it along but lost some friends,
And who is to say what it all meant.

But I can look into your eyes,
And see all the dreams you kept inside,
That were for only you to know,
And maybe they will never be shown.

I think this isn't who you want to be,
You just want to be free with me,

Free to be who you are inside,
Free to let your thoughts run wild.

Free enough so that you won't hide,
As free as the birds high in the sky,
This isn't who you want to be,
Show them what you want them to see.

After that I'll know

So don't walk away from my love,
Even if my love was never enough,
For you to truly see,
what I want us to be.

Cause once you've walked away,
I'll know it's finally too late,
For you to truly see,
What I wished we could have been.

You got me

You got me any way you want me,
If you want me at all,
You got me here and there,
You got me there and here,
Any way you want me,
Just let me go.

You got me any way you want me,
If you want me at all,
You got me up and down,
You got me down and up,
Any way you want me,
Just let me go.

You got me any way you want me,
If you want me at all,
You got me running and hiding,
You got me hiding and running,
Any way you want me,
Just let me go.

You got me any way you want me,
If you want me at all,
You got me back and front,
You got me front and back,
Any way you want me,
Just let me go.

You got me any way you want me,
If you want me at all,
You got me now and forever,
You got me forever and now,

Any way you want me,
Just let me go.

To victory

Here is the man into battle,
Straddled on horseback riding to the dry plains,
Sword at hand and victory in sight,
Racing ever forwards with 200 more at his side.

The horns are blown and horses churn the ground,
A chorus of screaming ensues as they charge never looking
back,
The leader instructs, with focus like an arrow,
"Onwards men allow them to meet their gods on this day".

But now they yell no more as the arrow heads pierce their
skins,
Their horses toppled and cracked down facing,
They have fallen like the autumn leaves from the trees,
They are past like rain hitting the mountain side.

There are no graves nor was there a song to be sung,
The grief stole that away as much as the sword that stole
their lives,
Their sun set on the, never to return,
Once great men cut down to nothingness.

Slow march of the horseman parading through the castle
streets,
The people throw flowers at their feet as they leave for
war,
None of them looking back at the families they're leaving
behind,
On the dry plains they march onwards.

The internet

The internet is a tool for mass communication around the
world,
But with that it also brings a lot of hate from information
that is tainted,
Causing in turn a lack of truth and understanding,
There are also those who are still clinging to old
normalities,
Which don't work anymore, not that they ever did,
If you can't fit with the new world of acceptance,
Then you'll die in your old world of judgment.

Life is getting faster

A lot of hard days lately,
And everyday is harder,
But no one makes it easy,
No ones working smarter.

Even though some days,
You never hear a good word,
They just can't afford to say,
That it's all you can pay to be heard.

But now life is getting faster,
And they're not on the right track,
They're looking for the answer,
But they all missed it way back.

And now there's not enough hours,
In any of the days,
Cause now it's all about getting power,
Though it's always been that way.

At the end of the day

Here's to us at the end of the day,
Thinking of being put to rest, in our beds that we lay,
With each other at arms standing tall,
For the chance of freedom we will give it our all.
Our lives were always meant to go this way.

Here's to us at the end of the day,
Thinking of being put to rest, in our beds that we lay,
The sound at the top of the trees is now dulled,
We have found new purpose that cannot be nulled,
Our lives will mean everything on this day.

Here's to us at the end of the day,
Thinking of being put to rest, in our beds that we lay,
Did all the glory go straight to our heads,
It doesn't matter who we are once we're dead,
Did our deaths mean anything anyway.

Someday

Someday all your woes will be lost in time,
And your present will be bliss and full of joy.

Chained to my misery

I am but a walking shadow of who I use to be,
An empty shell of my former self on display for all to see,
My shackles crack, chained to my misery,
Pulled am I, down to the depths of my self pity,
But justified is my sorrow as my tears could fill the sea,
The pain in my head overgrown and now it consumes me.

Work work work work work

You're a bemused face, almost only a blank expression,
Pale complexion coupled with an aimless stare,
Work till you die, the whole world is stressing,
And you'll never stop, so you'll have no time to care.

Past grievances

Keep your eyes to the ground,
Look down,
Look down,
Never to be found,
Look down,
Look down,
You can't hear a sound,
Look down,
Look down,
In the sea you'll be drowned,
Look down,
Look down,
To the chains you are bound,
Look down,
Look down,
Keep your eyes to the ground,
And look down.

Leaving

You can't blame anyone for leaving,
People need to worry about themselves before anyone
else,
As do you, worry about you and not about something you
can't control,
Some people are only meant to be in your life for a short
while anyways.

Tip toeing

Through this world you glide,
With love in your stride,
A graceful sight to see,
You are the one for me.

Take care of each other

I know we can all get too enthralled in our own lives,
Sometimes forgetting about other people's feelings,
But it's always best to be honest and keep it simple,
And so if you want a life with no complications,
Tell the people you love that you love them,
As often and as loudly as you can.

Here's to me and here's to you

Let our parting deaths be that of glory,
Let someone else retell of our story,
And still the words shall remain true,
And so I say, heres to me and here's to you.

Will my death just be one more death coming,
Is my life just another life that means nothing.

Will we be remembered for what we gave,
Will what we did echo past our graves,
And still the words shall always be,
And so I say, here's to you and here's to me.

No such thing

There is no such thing as too nice,
There is no such thing as too nice,
There is no such thing as too nice,
There is no such thing as too nice,
There is no such thing as too nice,
There is no such thing as too nice.

The stress of travel

Muffled tannoy system,
Running to catch the train,
Faces drenched in misery,
And stress befalling their brain.

Bars in your window

Living a lifetime of pain,
Screaming to break free of your chains,
Cause now your 'over the rainbow',
Has turned to bars in your window,
And you'll never be free again.

Who's in the wrong

As you sit in the calming silence of the sky,
Obsessing in your own head and wondering why,
It all worked out the way it did and if it was meant to be,
If what happened is what you needed to see.

"I'm not a racist but"

The wider public are not overtly racist,
Nor do they have racist tendencies,
But if you were to give them the chance,
If it means they'll be welcomed into a group,
If they'll be shown some form of community with their
peers,
They'll no doubt take that chance without a second
thought.

It doesn't matter if it's a racist song, joke or point of
reference,
If it means they'll get a laugh from the people around
them,
And to receive a laugh is to receive affection,
It's inevitable that they will turn on their inner hidden
prejudices,
Whether they're real suppressed feelings or a work of
fiction,
Is neither here nor there in this situation.

To be racist for the sake of a joke,
Is not only wrong but it is increasingly dangerous,
Because then it means that to hurt someone is something
to laugh about,
And that's where we drift apart from each other,
When in this world if we want peace,
We need to grow together with inclusions for all people.

Inner peace

I think it's nice to have some time out to yourself,
Painting, writing or taking a book from your dusty shelf,
Playing some music or even just sitting quietly on your
bed,
Thinking out revolutions and histories inside your own
head,
Do it now, as that time you take will never again be found,
You find out who you really are, when no one else is
around.

Still

You looked no bigger than a child,
Like a pale skinned angel,
But you left your body behind,
You were cold with your eyes shut,
That was the last time I saw you,
But that wasn't who you were.

You were as light as life itself,
You mixed your yellow hue into the grey backdrop of this
world,
You shone your light through to us all,
Making our dark skies bright,
That is who you were,
That is who you are still.

Drowning

A swirling sky alludes to a false sense of security,
As I drift into the storms of the open sea,
Struggling to stay afloat I panic helplessly,
Trying to wrestle with the waves as they rise above me.

The decision

Am I now seeing you in a different light,
Or have I got the full picture finally in sight,
As I stand before you knowing in my heart I don't love you,
While having to fake all the signs that I still do.

But the worst part is just before you're about to begin,
With that comfortable silence that you both sit in,
She's in love and you'd wish you felt it too,
Instead heartbreak will be caused by what you're about to
do.

You have to do it no matter how hard it will be,
And hopefully someday she too will be able to see it
clearly,
It seems that she's in love with someone who isn't real
anymore,
And this is not something I've had to deal with before.

Why don't we ever say what we really
mean,
Is it best to leave the emotions unseen,
keeping it simmering on the surface inside,
Allowing it to corrupt, weaken and erode your mind.

The feelings are gone

You can't love someone you don't,
You think it'll get better but it won't,
You can't love someone just because they love you,
And you can't let someone believe that you love them too.

A lifetime wasted

Don't ever work your whole lives,
Giving it all you got,
For just a couple weeks in the sunshine,
Just because it's hot.

I never wanted that to be mine,
It's not what I set for myself,
But you don't have a choice sometimes,
As you put your dreams on the back shelf.

Cause sometimes you have to,
Pay for the dreams you wasted,
And sometimes it makes you,
Feel a strange hatred.

For the life you're in now,
Breaking your back everyday,
And you'll undoubtedly wonder how,
You let your self settle this way.

Telling the truth isn't always a good idea

Alone,
with no home,
Your heart is worn,
Your mind is torn,
You walk the road,
But there's no where to go,

That bizarre silence

It's like knowing what it's like to be dead,
Growing up together but we have nothing to say,
Though I have full scripts in my head,
I didn't plan on it being this way.

Part IIII

Restricted and restrained minds,
But our human duty is to be free.

Under a nest of new born birds

Simply dressing your betrayal up as an emotional
renaissance,
Does not make it so,
And just because lying rewarded you,
Does not mean it worked out as it should,
And now I hear you're demanding to be treated special.

Love is like any creative practice, it has its own agonies,
It brings its own agonies with it when it arrives,
"I love you" she said, "I love you but I'm still leaving",
Our love made her lackadaisical,
When it was only ever meant to be a temperate thing.

Gratitude in a time to be grateful

It can go overlooked too passively just how many people
are demoralised,
Cut down too much to handle, dying from lack of
affirmative attention,
And how many are pained day by day starved for an
encouraging word,
And how easy it can be to administer such a word, if you're
careful with it,
You may think you don't have everything and it very well
may be true,
But if you can just sit down and breathe,
There are plenty of people who don't have that.

Dear our beloved Julia

Weighed down by our love, now meaning less,
And a lot of what we said, does not make sense,
I'd try again and again, for one more chance,
But I can't help but feel my place is somewhere else.

So I write to you with my heart ample in it's pain,
No more I want but to clutch you in my bosom and hold
you there till day,
But I say with bated breath I'm leaving once more again,
I swear I'll never forget you our beloved Julia.

The truth remains the truth

Our love has passed through our hands unchallenged,
And what we really need to say, continues to be unsaid,
Our mind keeps tight those such words,
But the truth remains the truth.

Only you

I don't want to be apart from it,
I want to be a part of it,
Spinning your heels off the floor of the gallery,
It's absurd just how perfect it can be,
Isn't it strange how natural it feels,
That all I want is you.

Closing remarks

The feeling that I'll never see you again can not be outgrown,
And I do declare I fear much of what is to come,
I would not have me turn into someone you don't talk about,
So every now and again may you think of me,
I want only for you to remember me, as I am.

Stay gone forever

My grief is nothing more than our love persisting,
And so I hope only for this grief to stay with me,
I'm still too in love with you to let you go from my
memory,
Nothing can stay gone forever.

Talk to me about the weather

Just sit with me a while,
Moments like this are few and far between,
Comfortable silence is a virtue,
Love stores many unexpected pleasures.

Blackbird

There is a blackbird festering away in my heart,
It's built it's nest,
It calls me it's home,
So here it doth stay,
There is a blackbird pecking away at my heart,
Sometimes it tries to get out of its cage,
But they tell me, I am made to be too strong for that to
happen,
And so I push him down even further,
There is a blackbird nesting itself in my heart,
And I am too embarrassed to tell anyone about him.

Words

All in lies whispers, now come to naught but a dusty death,
Words can be tower blocks, to build monuments to whom
that speaks them,
And then are washed away by the very wind they're sent
out from the mouth into,
Words can be great, words can be cruel, and words can be
nothing but words.

Women are not properties

Until the rightful standardisation
that one person has no more rights
then any other,
is fulfilled
and felt in all hearts
eternally
and without any question,
women will not know peace.

And until the current standardisation
that one person making choices
upon another persons body,
comes to a swift end
and isn't put to a vote
nationally
it needs no discussion,
all women deserve choice.

War

We're being lied to yet again,
Treat like dogs under the boot of those who say they
represent us,
Alls they do is laugh at us,
And everywhere there's wars.

What do we do then,
When we work our whole lives and don't even reap the
benefits of our labour,
Our lives are made to feel inferior,
And everywhere there's wars.

So when will it stop,
We need to stop letting men make choices on behalf of
other peoples bodies,
Woman are not properties,
And everywhere there's wars.

And what about us,
Being lead from the back, into submission and force us to
be silent and behave,
They broke the rules they made,
And everywhere there's wars.

There's no more room now,
Under the weight of the power our individuality is
suppressed,
They took our creative prowess,
And everywhere there's wars.

So who are they to say,
Why is it up for debate and a vote on who can love who,

It has nothing to do with you,
And everywhere there's wars.

They'll never see another day,
Friends take the life they should be living right now, it's
too many too soon,
Phantom faces in the room,
And everywhere there's wars.

The pain doesn't stop,
In our heads even though it's the hardest battle to fight, it
never ends,
Here it comes again,
And everywhere there's wars.

Money is the answer,
If you wish to be miserable live a life based around it's
pursuit,
Money is the root,
And everywhere there's wars.

Some are bigger then others,
Do they think about the children crying while they watch
as their parents die,
They didn't even get to say goodbye,
And everywhere there's wars.

And for what is the point of it,
Incinerating a country in the name of war now you're just
king of the rubble,
But you won't take the people,
And everywhere there's wars.

Across the seas,
One day the international morality shall bring forth a new
future of equality,
Soon we'll all be free,
But for now everywhere there's wars.

Lean on a dream of us

Every night to soothe my weary soul to sleep,
I lay there and lean on a dream of you,
Every time when I feel myself getting in too deep,
I lay there and lean on a dream of you,
Or when it's all falling down I have no strength to keep,
I lay there and lean on a dream of you,
And so I want you to know, I love you endlessly,
Just be here and lean on a dream of me.

The last sibling left

Rosy cheeked, hazel eyes, first day of summer at the beach,
Ice cream in the hot weather, water balloon fights,
5 including me, 7 all in a 3 bedroom house,
The boys room and the girls room next door to each other,
Our parents couldn't have gotten more different kids,
School runs were the hardest part, as we fight over the
front seat,
But we all wait for each other to walk home together,
Then we come of age, go off and get married,
And still we come round for dinner, telling stories of our
childhood together,
New houses, children, Christmas, Easter and birthdays,
The odd phone call just to check in.

Then life moves on.

And the phone rings no more,
Those pictures hang there only with faded souls in them,
The stories are all worn out, told too many times,
The lively flower now turns sad,
The young boy turns into an old man, and cries alone,
He looks to himself and ponders,
Why should I be expected to smile,
When everyone who has ever loved me has died.

And still I sit still

The opportunities come into my reach,
One after another they go,
And still I sit still.

The days end, the nights begin again,
One after another they go,
And still I sit still.

Summer breeze and winters chill,
One after another they go,
And still I sit still.

Lovers have my heart until they break it,
One after another they go,
And still I sit still.

Missed calls from friends sitting still by their phones,
One after another they go,
And still I sit still.

Juxtaposed, heavy mind, enlightened ideas,
One after another they go,
And still I sit still.

My entire life is passing me by, so fast it doth go,
And still I sit still.

Friday nights for fine dining

Friday nights for fine dining,
Ladies and gentlemen at their tables,
Eating small food for big money,
Cheap wine with an expensive name,
The piano man plays in a rented suit,
Performing a song he doesn't like,
Singing words he didn't write,
On a piano he doesn't own.

And the ladies and gentlemen just continue to talk and eat
and laugh.

Clinking, spitting, chewing, plotting and planning,
Powering over the sound of a second hand Steinway,
Missing a note but there was no concern,
The piano mans face was bare, pale and sickly looking,
His head had a bag over it,
His fingernails needed cut,
His hair needed cleaned,
He excuses himself for a break, as he gets up to no
applause.

And the ladies and gentlemen just continue to talk and eat
and laugh.

Passing waiters in the dining room with holes in the souls
of their shoes,
Opening the bathroom door to find the cocaine lines,
Sitting alone in a locked stall, pleased no one can see him,
As he looks down, with his head in his hands, at his shoes,
He notices a small drain under his foot on the floor,
And sidles at it with a pleasant relief,

And then he shot himself in the head,
And what's left of him trickles down the small drain under
his foot.

And the ladies and gentlemen just continue to talk and eat
and laugh.

Perfume

The argon is afloat and I pass through its vacuum too,
Now bequeathed it's scent, with yours in its place,
Subtle and soft, the air tastes of you,
Beguiled have I been, out of touch no more.

Binds me still

I see the thunder in the sky, the swirling of the storm,
Covering the birds flying by, above the sun that took the form,
Clouded by your reach is my world, now under surveillance,
Shrouded by the touch of a girl, I waited for with patience,
You have started a precedence, in my heart now holding me here,
For it is a mighty bird of pestilence, that flies into my ear,
Your voice I had not heard, and yet desperately I sought it,
Your mouth then speaks the word, and yet I had not caught it,
And all of this I welcome for good or for ill,
And all that you are binds me still.

The last conversation

I would never ask you not to cry, as crying is remembering.

I hope this grief stays with me, it is nothing more then all the love i couldn't express.

Although it feels as if we never really got a chance at it.

I am grateful still, some people don't even get as long as we did.

It's true that the few years with you, was to me, the most precious point in history.

And I'm glad too of the time I had with you, as loving someone is truly living.

I would never ask you not to cry, as crying is remembering.

And not all tears have to be tears of despair.

Red and blue

Driving along the country roads with a blood red coloured
sky,
Soon to be drowned out by that deeper blue, that matches
both our eyes,
Swirling around the corners with my hand placed upon
your thigh,
And that look upon your face, not quite love, but it can get
me by.

Don't knock me down cause you've been building me brick
by brick,
Your hands around my neck and mine stroking that small
tattoo on your hip,
Taste of fruit on your tongue and look of lust glued to your
lips,
You're as fine as wine, and all I've ever wanted to do was
to take a sip.

Heated kitchen floor warming our clothes thrown down as
we lie there after sex,
What can we say, I guess, it just happens in the places that
we least likely expect,
As it always does but we're not in control of any of it,
I hope you don't mind me saying that, I don't mean to
cause you disrespect.

I can't help but be obsessed with you, your voice sounds so
sweet to me,
You sound just like a song, soothing me in all the ways I
wish to be,
I don't mind if you want to chain me up cause from you I
don't want to be free,

I don't even mind if you wish to leave, I will still hold you in my heart, with sincerity.

We talked for hours and hours and we danced on the forest floor,
The nights were full of life we didn't have a clue what was in store,
You blossomed for me like a flower and shocked me straight to my core,
My only wish is that we had stayed there, even just for a few moments more.

Driving back on the country roads with a blood red coloured sky,
Soon to be drowned out by that deeper blue that matches both our eyes,
Swirling around the corners with my hand placed upon your thigh,
And that look upon your face, not quite love, but it can get me by.

All I want is you

You're a fresh face clearing the mist of a new English
morning,
The golden brown needle piercing through the blackened
skies of dawn,
Forthwith, I was consumed with the idea my heart would
break once more,
But with your smile, as it is in such a way, you make the
whole world take notice,
Before you, she who slept a year by my side, my heart
never truly grasped,
And yet with you, I can't help but hang onto even just the
words you say,
It would be foolish of me to deny what my heart already
knows,
When I hold you in my arms, and I feel my finger on your
trigger,
It's clear to me, that all I want is you.

Do you really think they'll drop the bombs

In the small hours of the night when the whole worlds asleep,
The flickering match of destructive intention now turns to ignite the flames of war,
The siren calls, the stars fall, the wall that divides starts to crumble,
Now it's open warfare, for the blood to be spilt,
The mass staining of white lining sheets, there is a street bound fire fight,
Get out of your seats for it's the end of the world,
Midnight brawls, augmented with the screams of innocent children,
Cowering in fear, unaware their parents can no longer save them,
The bombs drop in the small hours of the night, and now no one is asleep.

Sweet waters salted

There's a great pain behind your eyes of veiled favour,
I see that she has infected your dreams once more,
She too has infected mine once before,
The maiden, so fair, so harsh not to stay in,
Her soft hide betwixt her wings of lilac silk,
Fluttering, fluttering so fast it is as if they were not there,
Through her twisted caramel curtains that hang over her
eyes, she watches,
In young men's ears as they drift off to vacant slumber, she
whispers,
She speaks words that to only the young man are known,
And then they sleep and dream their quiet dreams of love,
Or for what she tells them true love is,
And so now their heads are filled with white noise,
A constant ringing that for nought can prevail it to stop,
Her beauty may only be surface deep,
But her words strike even the strongest to sleep,
She is alike and yet unlike any of whom she resembles,
A ponderous creature that from under her hair she looks,
And what she sees is you,
And what you see is love.

Our scene

We have no say on life moving forward,
All we can do is contribute to its texture,
As we, the characters, die, are replaced and forgotten,
The play still unfolds, the action still happens,
All we can do is hope to contribute our scene.

Bluebird

Every stranger has a story to tell,
Everyone has a broken heart,
There are small moments in life that make everyone smile,
But everyone has a broken heart.

World appeal

(There's nothing complicated about it)

This is the world appeal.

"Money is ever so valuable for myself and for you",
But it's only worth is people give it value,
In the pursuit of money we are forced to make choices,
In the real world money drowns out our voices.

Store some in a box for harder times,
Cause we're never paid anything for writing rhymes,
Money is necessary come what may,
And yet you feel no different come pay day.

This world can make enemies into friends,
People will use you as a means to an end,
We are taught about money in our school classrooms,
But not how much is burnt in nuclear mushrooms.

We scramble around picking pennies for luck,
We replace our humanity with a selfish conduct,
And nowadays the youth are all looked down on,
By the older who don't realise they're where we came
from.

But this man coverts that man converting a third man
converting the first,
And that mans coming down on his luck his mental decline
is at its most worst,
So why don't we talk about the 1 in 12 dying for nothing,
It's always too late till you wish you'd done something.

Remember to spare a moment of your day to the friends
who didn't make it,
Those who put on a brave face until it's too much to fake it,
And what about for here and now what do we do,
When we can't even agree on what's true.

Take some of that money that you haul,
And give it to the man on the street so he doesn't fall,
Under the upper hand with his cold feet,
Give him enough just so he can eat.

And what's sad is he was told to be glad,
That he's alive even with the little that he has,
He finds a place to sleep till he's told to move on by the
police,
It's no surprise he's an addict it's chipping away at him
piece by piece.

It isn't a bad thing the people in this country change,
But what we can't have is people who think the new
people look strange,
Racism is the cause of a lot of this worlds violence,
Never miss a good opportunity for it to be silenced.

Go on a protest march and stand up for the rights,
For everyone just to be able to sleep safe at night,
It's not hard if you want to feel good at the end of the day,
Then all you need to do is give all that money away.

When we were born we were made to listen to what they
said,
We were told to abandon the ideas that we had in our
head,

Boys can be girls and girls can be boys, don't listen to their hateful pride,
Identity means fluidity, the only thing that matters is what we feel on the inside.

But what good is it,
If no one is saying,
The truth that matters,
When the worlds in tatters,
Friends are dying,
Lovers are lying,
While the world is crying,
Politicians are betraying,
Church folk are praying,
But what we all need is to come together,
What we all need more love for each other.

Now I just want to see this, so we don't all feel so forsaken,
I just want to see the light in this world before it gets taken.

This is the world appeal.

The sky isn't falling

The sky isn't falling but I can't help but feel we're finally all under attack,
The sky isn't falling but the light in their heads are starting to go black,
The sky isn't falling but in your heart you know you may never get back,
The sky isn't falling but that doesn't mean you can't see it start to crack.

Alone

Friends have my heart and their turmoil has my attention
for it's own,
And yet for all the love I give to them,
I am alone.

The good deeds for the sake of them, that to no one else
were known,
And yet for all the kindness I have in my heart,
I am alone.

Restless I am, to begin work again, my back aches to the
bone,
And yet for all the hard work given to the company,
I am alone.

Relationships gone by once more, but the feelings are not
yet outgrown,
Although I hold no ill will to those who I once loved,
I am alone.

Walking the December streets as the snowflake littered air
is blown,
And in the coldest winter nights it's clearer, than any
other, to me,
I am alone.

And all the melancholy of this world be then manifested
within the same tone,
And so day by day from birth to death, comes only one
truth,
I am alone.

Too much,
We want for, too much.

Modern day presence on your shoulder

Love is a pill from a bottle made synthetically,
While our lips are out of sync with our heart,
Beaty is measured on a handheld screen, romance is
technology,
And these days who the hell even cares about art.

Be kind- final part (extended)

Even after all the dark in this world, there's enough power
still to lift up your head,
Care not for war or violence and talk to your enemies
instead,
Think not of nuclear weaponry, no amount of hate can
stop all the love,
Choose kindness every time you can and never forget the
ones left above.

Much like our loved ones already, all things must pass
after a little while,
But have no fear for what is to come because none of us
can stop the times,
Life keeps moving forward, we either waste it or make the
most,
Hold tight to your memories with family, and think on the
feeling they evoke.

Do not let your politicians dissuade you, they only
encourage divided lines,
Stand up for what you believe, and stay clear with decisive
minds,
I see my friends and remember, life is always worth living,
Life is made for love and transgressions done by the
desperate should be forgiven.

Before this everywhere I went lead me to where I didn't
want to be,
Try to tell us different if you want, but it's our wholly
nature to be free.

Pain killers on the nightstand

Going down stairs to make a cup of tea,
Walking past the bathroom door and stop at the top
landing,
The Christmas decorations were out in full force once
more,
Met at the top of the stairs without a greeting, his face was
different,
Not just pale on the surface but sickly behind the eyes,
He didn't say a word, I'm not even sure if he looked at me,
He just picked up a snow globe that was set on the
window sill,
Grasping in his hands to admire it then twisting the crank
at the base,
Putting it back in its place with a melancholy Christmas
tune,
A nightmarish ring,
And as I passed him walking down the stairs I had this
feeling,
Something had just happened in the bathroom,
I knew he wasn't well but you never expect it to be
serious,
You don't think it'll ever happen until it does,
If I didn't see this it would have been like any other
morning.

Walking back up, the bathroom door was closed again,
And all that was heard was the snow globe, it just kept on
playing.

6:23 in the morning, and I can't remember if it's real

Lately the memories we shared keep coming back to me,
And I find myself letting them linger there for a few
moments more each time,
Because i often wonder what if that's the last I'll ever see
them,
So I savour the moment, trying to bring life back to what is
already gone,
But when I think of them, they always seem to fade a little
more,
So that now I can't remember if they're even a real
memory at all.

Everything could change in a moment

It's not talked about enough how it can all be gone In a
moment,
Everything you were, all you had ever wanted to be,
Gone like snowflakes melting on the ground, never to be
seen again,
Never to be repeated in the same way and never to be
reversed.

The secrets that were only to yourself known, they'd
remain unshared,
The aspirations, the plans you kept putting off, the
thoughts of the future,
All of them would fade into internal whispers in time,
never to be heard,
Any moment could be that last moment, and it only takes a
moment to come.

Never again

No ones heart has the same feelings yours does,
No ones eyes can see the world quite like you can,
No ones hands touches the world in a way that feels the same,
And no ones mind creates the same dreams twice.

They all grow up to be like one who they knew

Iona McCarthy,
Planting the seeds in the garden hoping that one day
they'll grow,
It all moves too slow,
Sat in her arm chair,
Watching the old paper peel, on her living room walls,
No body calls.

Elijah Arima,
Typing away at her papers due to hand in next week,
Life seems so bleak,
The look on her face shows,
Nothing but stress from the things that she doesn't know,
Where does she go.

Iona McCarthy,
Died in her home but for her funeral no body came,
The day was unchanged,
Elijah Arima,
Grew up to be nothing like her dreams and now she too
lives alone,
She just waits by phone.

180909

Do you dream in colour,
Do you feel like you're alone,
Do you fill your nights with wonder,
Are you just trying to get back home.

An exercise in keeping alive

Street lights, felt unsafe,
Sunken eyes, tired face,
Shes never asked for her name,
Same clothes, makeup,
The cold winds start taking her,
Upon her face, a lonely pain.

Fell onto hard times,
Long days, longer nights,
Razor blade sawn to her thighs,
Walk the streets, smiling,
In the mirror, crying,
Tears run black from her eyes.

Park bench, rain fall,
No friends, missed calls,
Cool girl, no where to go,
By herself, all day,
China white-shore holiday,
Her feet freeze from the fallen snow.

Packs herself in another car,
Hotel room, 2 star,
She sits up waiting for the sun to rise,
Plastic heart, paper lungs,
Another round has begun,
Same routine, no surprise.

The nightshift

Riding home on the bus, clocked off for the night,
Damp clothes, from the dive, £1.70 for a single ticket,
Going home to sleep from a hard nights work,
Waiting to do it again, another shift at 10,
Burn marks, blistered feet, from shoes falling apart,
Payday at midnight during work hours,
But the money doesn't make you feel any different,
And yet we keep on working for it,
I'm thinking of taking up smoking so I can get a few smoke breaks,
Rude customers, incompetent staff, there's nothing good about it,
They don't know what it's like to work the nightshift here.

Fretless, witless, pointless

Fretless, witless wonders be over our heads,
Don't we all yearn for something greater than what is
lived,
A countryside house overlooking water running,
Or a job that we love, so we would never have to work
again.

So what have we to do but to shackle ourselves to the 9 to
5,
Our self worth is cuffed to ideas of duty and responsibility,
Requested time is a trick, we do not owe ourselves to
labouring force,
Our lives are measured in work, our time is paid for.

Restricted and restrained minds, but our human duty is to
be free.

A lake by the side of the sea

Beaded sweat running races, once cold bathroom tiles,
now steaming,
The window was kept closed only in this room of the
house,
Dead flies on the sill of the window, they couldn't escape
either,
Bent over the bathtub or up against the wall.

Punishment from a creature bigger than you are,
Does it make him feel more like a man or lesser,
Horses bite gripped to my leg to keep me in place,
Buckles, metal, noises, tears and screaming.

I'll either do this to my own or I'll live alone,
Did his do the same to him, he must have learnt this from
someone,
He's a bastard, he's nothing but a coward as much as I'll
be,
He taught me many things, and all of them bad.

At the end the only words that are spoken are words
behind the eyes,
As your mother looks at you, then to your father, then
back at you,
She says that she's okay with this,
I didn't scream the next time, and that was the last time it
happened.

this is not a true story

Everyday lives of the lonely people

I walked down a street one night, a street I didn't know,
Down towards the back alleys, where the lonely people
are found,
The streets were full of people, some smiling and some
not,
But all with a face that you could see had a story behind it.

Simple pleasures of a cigarette and a cup of coffee,
Sitting out in front of the house waiting for something to
happen,
The promise of the city life with none of the realities,
Everyday people living everyday lives, everyday.

Cracks in the pavement, potholes and telephone wires,
Birds picking up the scraps of food left out for the
neighbourhood dogs,
Faded yellow lines painted on the road,
Faded dreams lost to 'getting on with your life'.

Unkept grass from the elderly couple in the middle of the
street,
Their wall paper is an eyesore, yellow mustard flowers on
a black wall,
You can see it through gaps in the curtains, they always
keep shut,
Like it's their way of ignoring the world as it passes them
by.

Teenage lovers walking home from a night on the town,
Passing me by and stumbling into the road, walking, hands
holding,

Making it to their stop, the drainpipe hanging off from the wall,
Spilling water down onto the street outside their house.

The sun sets covering itself with the far away hill on the horizon,
And the moon shines it's frosted white glow on the houses,
Seeing your breathe whistle out from your mouth, like a steam train,
I scrape my boots along the pavement as I walk, getting to where I'm going.

Street lamps flickering, most not even working,
A beaten up bus stop with graffiti tags over and over again,
It's quiet after dark but for the family down the road with screaming kids,
A street full of lonely people, I don't know where they all come from.

Cycles

Everything comes around in cycles,
What you were, you'll see in another,
And you'll realise you are now someone else you knew
before,
The phases of life repeat over and over,
The same actions, the same reactions,
The same people, the same situations,
Everything comes around in cycles.

So much more

No parent should ever have to bury their children,
No one ever prepares you for this type of situation,
Clothes unworn, days un-lived, so much time wasted,
But my days with you, to me, I hold them sacred.

The flowers set out on your grave, will grow in your stead,
Your room given over to the dust along with your last
unmade bed,
A room so quiet you can hear the walls age over time,
A heart so lonesome now that you are no longer mine.

She

She keeps her hands inside silk gloves,
One for each to show her class,
The skin of a turtle dove,
Clutching onto a wine glass,
Falling for her effortlessly,
She speaks so impeccably,
She's always so extraordinarily refined.

She comes alive in the dance halls,
Not likely denied invitations,
Learnt on cigarettes and alcohol,
A book for each situation,
Charmer at the dining room,
And darker in the bedroom,
But still extraordinarily refined.

Recommended at a price,
She draws you in with her smile,
Slight of hand, gold delight,
Impeccable in every style,
It's known to all she's well read,
Fresh linings aligning every bed,
Cause she's extraordinarily refined.

What's the harm to flirt sometimes,
She's often asked about it,
Going out while she's in her prime,
Who wants to know about her,
"She says hey big spender,
You're a New York pretender",
She's always extraordinarily refined,

You are born into this world

The first thing you learn is to cry,
You're brought into this world, then you die,
You are a singular person, to yourself be true,
You were born into this world just to be you.

Caught up in the blues for today i sit alone

I know your mind rests so heavy in your lonesome room,
And I would have given you my all, if it was enough to help
you through,
But for now I rest easy knowing we are both under the
same moon,
And that someday soon I won't have to go the nights
without seeing you.

Same old same old

I'm not the type of man who often likes to socialise,
I seem to find myself running the same old races,
And I see myself in all of the good times that I had over the years,
All the good times I had had with all the familiar faces.

The world is a funny farm

Here and watch the sight of the dogs that come to beat,
The pig pens have unleashed their servings on the sheep,
Injustice makes everyday a little more bleak,
As the fresh buds are crumbling more and more each
week.

Food scraps from their plates, the pigs mistreat,
Even though for every one pig, there's a thousand sheep,
Day by day nothing will ever come of the weak,
As the sheep have not even the power enough to speak.

I saw a white dog he was hunting a black sheep,
Protect the neck from the boots edge placed deep,
The dogs follow orders and kiss the pigs muddy feet,
And every so often the pigs will throw their dogs a treat.

Stepping over and getting larger the pigs continue to peak,
Fresh dinner jackets, awaiting their newly hunted meat,
Around the animal farm they take their high horse seats,
Hungry for more the pigs are here ready to eat.

Here and watch the sight of the dogs that come to beat,
With not enough food for the sheep to eat,
And only once the sheep wise up and unleash,
All we will hear is the big pigs speak.

Wake no more

How can I not live my life in fear,
When life to us all is something we know not of,
We know not but for what our eyes and our minds may
deem true,
We have no idea what it is that we live for.

At the beginning life was long,
Your mind growing and expanding as much as your body,
Teaching your tongue to talk so it may reveal first words,
Until then you finish growing by the time you reveal your
love for someone.

The young mans game is being played,
Love and heartbreak bookend your final stages of youth,
No one could possibly understand the complexities of you,
No one could ever understand all of your hidden truths.

Until you meet that one person,
And life without them was like preparing for an exam,
You were getting ready for your real life to finally come to
fruition,
But in doing so you missed that your life had already
began.

Appointments made more frequent as you sleep more
then before,
Grey hair, aching bones and shaking hands plague you,
When you forgot the name of your first love, the hurt
never left you,
Seeing the same faces over and over once you wake.

And then you wake no more.

How can I not live my life in fear,
When life to us all is something we know not of,
We know not but for what our eyes and our minds may
deem true,
We have no idea what it is that we live for.

Rumours

You drop pebbles and it ripples in the well,
You drop names and the rumours will swell,
You drop friends, at the drop of a hat,
You drop from the screen and never come back.

Someone else

I know not the face of any one man,
And so I ponder if it is just you yourself,
I am what you think I am,
But I am also someone else.

The dreamer

A man is more awake when he dreams,
For in dreams he sees what is to come,
What is to come for he and his life,
Only to succeed in his dream means his real life will have
begun.

To dream is to live a life that is full of euphoria,
Dreams revive the human heart to beat strong,
The heart beats none-stop for the dreamer not to lose
hope,
And man cannot wait for his dream for too long.

Moral virtue

To aim to always see the good in people is a great virtue,
But you can't let that way of seeing, blind you to their truth,
Blind you to the other aspects of a person that can be harmful or dangerous,
There are too many people in this world who are not who they say they are.

Willem Avenue

I would walk alone on winter nights until I could hear no
noise at all,
Quiet streets leaving nothing but a drained streetlamp,
I go looking for the places no one else would go, searching
for silence,
Hearing nothing but for the beckoning of street walkers,
on Willem avenue.

Sometimes their beds would be the only thing that would
sooth a weary soul,
Always calling when you need a loving hand to help you
through,
I do admit there were some nights so cold I found some
warmth with them,
Allowing me to sleep and dream my solemn dreams of
you.

My broken heart still has a pulse, and my sorrow is not yet
laid to rest,
And so I shuffle down to the bar to break my woes with
another glass or two,
But it can't be helped, that all my emotions spill like the
drink laid to the floor,
And it's not selfish of me to simply want to see you smile
once more.

After leaving my home and my family I can't help but feel
regret,
Over the people I left behind, trying to chase something
that wasn't even mine,

But I digress, a man has to stick with his decisions, standing by his words alone,
Or he has nothing, nothing but for his empty promises stuck to his name.

Walking on, I think out loud thoughts that to only myself are known,
That to be be left alone is a virtue that some of us can't get easily,
I do suspect that those who can avoid being seen, by most the world, they will,
In a world that makes sense only to a few, it's not unusual to want to disappear.

And I'm tired of sitting in rooms full of talking with no conversation being had,
It seems as though people are so scared now, to open up to the ones they love,
And after years upon years of changing the same truths are still felt,
And it's clear that we are all still more or less the same.

Revolution is not a revelation

For years there seems to be the same words flowing
through the air,
The desire for revolution is not a revelation it has already
been felt,
Woe to those who make our lives something that isn't fair,
Mercy is still not shown to those who were disregarded
and forcefully knelt.

The Higher does whatever they can to bring about their
own greed,
Their hubris causing more pain until it's too much to
handle,
With not enough money there are some children we cant
even feed,
The lives of The Lower are not chips waiting for you to
gamble.

How many more have to suffer, and how many more
people have to die,
For change to finally be granted to those less fortunate,
Disbanding protests trying to make sure that we can't ask
them why,
But tell me this, why should I ever trust the government.

I am leaving once more again

I'm sorry for what I did to you,
And I'm sorry for all the heartbreak I caused,
For the pain you felt on those lost nights you had to face,
When I left you alone to cry to no one but yourself.

The night that everything ended,
I'm glad we're okay but I keep having this guilty feeling,
And it never leaves me in the moments that I think of you,
I'm not sure I'll ever be without those feelings again.

I still want you around even if it won't be like it was
before,
And I just want you to know that I still love you,
Just not like I did, although it's still a strong love I bare,
Full of sincerity and honesty and this I swear to you a
million times over.

It was true that at one time I thought you were the one for
me,
But we know these things they just happen,
And it's not always someone fault but we just have to deal
with it,
And make the best out of a bad situation for us both.

The man within

There is apart of me,
That is unknown even to myself,
I cannot figure out where it comes from,
But I know it's face.

Everyday conversation

Observe everyday conversation and you'll soon realise,
Most of what we all talk about is the past,
Is it because we find comfort in what we know,
And what we fear most is what is yet to come.

I should have just stayed at home

There once was a sleepy old in,
Unlike any I'd ever been,
They had drinks never seen before,
So much stuff I had to drink more,
And get so drunk it was obscene.

As more people arrived in the inn,
What we needed was a song,
The man in the corner started clapping his hands,
He says get up so we all had to stand,
And the night went on and on.

A few rhymes here in an off set key,
With a couple tunes in between,
Clapping and stomping as the glasses were clinking,
On their feet you could see that everyones singing,
When blue started dancing with green.

A man with a fiddle came knocking on the door,
In a jacket and his favourite hat,
So he played his fiddle with a penny in the middle,
And his band they started with their silly old skiffle,
And the dogs danced with the cats.

So the man with the fiddle continued to play,
A noise that would wake the dead,
The hour grew late and the landlord mad,
He felt things were getting way out of hand,
It's time for bed he said.

But they didn't care they paid no mind,
As they all danced upon the floor,

Raise a glass than they twist and spin,
Another round in this merry old inn,
They all just screamed for more.

Oh, Kicking stomping on the floor,
The inn is going to break,
As they jump around kicking to the sky,
Their legs are flying way up high,
Oh for goodness sake.

Says the landlord there behind the bar,
As he looses all control,
Chairs are breaking as dawn is waking,
And all you hear is the landlord saying,
I should have just stayed at home.

Embrace

We cannot hold onto memories,
We can only hold tight those we make memories with,
So embrace the ones who mean the most to you,
It shall remind you what is most important.

My mind is in bloom

My mind is in bloom and all I have to do is think of her,
And I will cast a million words away onto the page,
She will live forever in the words I have written,
Even after all the things we use to be start to fade away.

Hatred hidden behind a veil

You're a new summers morning, but with winters air still
lingering in the wind,
You send a chill to all those who drift out into the false
sunshine that you emit,
And I wish only to breathe the weightless air once more
for myself,
So why then when it rains, does it rain only on my house
alone.

Your skin is laced with deception while your eyes leave
them blind,
Your true self was once veiled, hidden behind your face
lined in sincerity,
But now the cloth that you once wrapped me in, hangs
only by a thread,
Even if you are still beautiful, I can see your soul is filled
only with hatred.

The dust has set on the harsh words that you said, now
living in my heart,
And after your storm raged through, forming my skies into
darkness,
And rising the waves around me devouring my every
waking moment,
That was when I saw who you really were behind all the
falsehoods.

There was once a time I drifted lazily in the pools of the
words you said,
Until the very essence of love was unceremoniously cast
aside,

And still were I not to know you, I would think there was love to salvage,
But I know there's nothing here, because there's nothing more that I see in you.

Lonely heart in a full bed

I turn my back on you in the bed,
You place your hand on my shoulder,
Why is nothing ever simple.

I felt nothing

Why is it that you were crying in my arms and I felt
nothing,
I said nothing except empty words that never meant
anything,
I made nothing except promises I knew would never be
kept,
I don't understand why I felt nothing as you wept.

Don't buy me all the things you think I want in an effort to
keep me,
Don't do all the things you think I want thinking that's who
I want you to be,
No matter how tight you hold onto my hand, my heart has
already let go of you,
Too much has changed now and I can't pretend to love
someone I no longer do.

There is no perfect moment to say goodbye for the last
time.

A box full of happiness

I once found a box full of pictures,
Reminding me of all of the things that we use to do,
And with my life I shall keep all of the ones of you safe,
So over and over I could relive my forgotten days with
you.

Hours

I wish only that we had more time,
Or at least that there were more hours in a day,
Because soon the sand runs out of the hourglass,
And we've wasted all of our time away.

And always I wish I could find the perfect set of words,
For what it is that I really want to say,
Because i know I can never make you understand,
As to why you make my heart feel this way.

And I wish that you were so much closer,
Closer than where it is that you stay,
Because you would be here safely in my arms,
And I promise I'd never lead you astray.

But life is what happens when you don't pay attention,
And now I have only these few moments to say,
That precious to me is every hour I was with you,
And I would have never had it any other way.

Can't find the right words

I wish my words weren't written so literal,
And I wish my emotions were a lot more versatile,
I still don't think I've done as good as I'm capable,
Nor have I done anything that I'd deem acceptable.

We're not the same

I'll never again love you as much as I do in my memories,
But now even those memories are slipping through my
hands,
Although standing in front of me, you look just as you once
did,
You're not the same one that walked away all those years
ago,
And so I now finally realise, everything changing on the
outside,
Changed everything that we were on the inside.

Rising waters

As I awake from an uneasy slumber on this night in mid
November,
At the sound of deep thunder I was rattled from visions of
the past,
Drifting off to sleep softly but I can't help but rise again
sharply
And I fiercely notice the hours don't pass me by as fast.

Blinds twisting, no light emitting, alone by the window
sitting,
And hourly the night grows later permitting the darkness
to consume,
My body feels hollow, dried skin and eyes sunk shallow,
I'm once more left till the morrow with not but the things
in my room.

And sat was I not talking, but in my head I was walking,
Strutting and stalking along the lone corridors of my brain,
A thousand words playing in my head abruptly stopping
me from staying in bed,
With terrors in my peace's stead, I spend yet another night
wide awake again.

Familiar scenes and images made up from dreams,
On nights like this one they soulfully seem to both alike
haunt me to my core,
And twisting obscurely they do my tongue and so forth the
nightmare comes,
And all I can wish upon is for the rising of the sun once
more.

But the night lasts ever longer and my fears grow ever stronger,
Causing them to conquer me more than they had done before,
The lamp by the window brightens as my chest harshly tightens,
So tight that my breathing rapidly increases with might therefore.

Avoiding my attack of panic and my thoughts of manic,
I sit calmly reading to soothe the heaviness felt in my soul,
Looking at myself from without I'm now steady and hold no wavering doubt,
That for now I have taken my panic under my control.

And yet my heads space is still cluttered and as I softly mutter,
And incoherently utter words that to not a soul they would be able to hear,
The sky keeps on pouring and the storms crescendo begins roaring,
My mind matched the mood of the brooding sky, greatly unclear.

My street now under water corroding the sunken bricks and mortar,
I lock myself away in horror so the rain can't get in from the windows edge,
All I do is watch from my room screaming at the sight of the water streaming,
Having to catch myself from leaning so far over the window ledge.

Reading to distract myself from the rising storm I pray for relief to form,
And protect me from the dangers swarming that won't clear,
Sifting through the pages fumbling as my mind begins crumbling,
I bead sweat with my bumbling face flushed in fear.

Or shall I allow myself to swallow the water till I wallow in it never seeing tomorrow,
And I would at last leave these torturous nights behind,
But then I remember I have no need to surrender,
Once I again realise, this is merely taking place inside my own mind.

The stranger at your door

As they stand at your door, you spit on the immigrants
shoes,
You of all people would do that to them,
The ones who at the very least should welcome them in,
Who should not make their lives any harder then what has
already been done,
It's different to hear a story, and then to see for your own
eyes,
Imagine you saw these people, lumbering along, hearts
bleeding,
Their babies crying as much as their babies are dying.

You sit watching their plight and you laugh at them,
From your crooked throne, sitting above all decency, you
laugh at them,
But what have you got,
What have you got that was earned and not stolen,
Democracy? No,
Riches? No,
Labour? No,
This place was made by the very same that you want to
throw out,
And as they lament, why are you enthused,
As they lament, why are you enthused.

Give one man more then another and he shall feed on his
friends like a hound,
Grant them removed if you are so sure that the self same
will not happen to you,
Were the circumstances changed would your hearts and
minds change with them,

If you were the so called ratchet immigrant how would
you be treated,
And so to then, where would you go,
Were you travel to France, Spain, New Zealand,
Anywhere that would grant you a safe bed,
Would your assured anger turn into pleads of mercy.

As you put down the strangers, as you rip their babies
from their mothers arms,
As you beat them in their staggered stride,
As you may even come to kill them once they should
approach too close,
As you turn them back to whence they came,
To a certain death, of that, you know you have done,
And then you look directly into your actions and see no
issue befalling them,
Leaving all sacred humanity cast down like the beginnings
of a plague,
And once you have done so that, then you are truly evil,
You have become the very thing you are so sure you are
abolishing.

Can you not instead cleft down onto your knees and bring
one up from sorrow,
Take in the stranger, share in his woes that with a careful
word may soon be relieved,
With the hands you use to hurt may you use to heal,
And may your words hold no such ill as it has done before,
The relationship with the text is one of immersion and not
domination,
So instead speak with a melody only to soothe,
Reach out your hand for peace, to those who are different,
And may you help the stranger at your door.

Part v

A heart that leads with love is never lost.

Sonnet 50: too little too late

Bright days came but they did not for long last,
Your bubble is burst, the dreams are all gone,
You cling now to what is already past,
Trying with all your will just to hold on.

So is it just finally you can see,
That no one can know what it really means,
Who you are is not who you wished to be,
You now realise it's too late for your dreams.

Staring at the night sky wishing on stars
Drop a penny for the man on the moon,
No one, but he said "it won't be too far",
And he said "you will have all your dreams soon".

But life flew past you with no time to wait,
And you realised it, too little too late.

Sonnet 51: deep scars

To open my eyes and see you each morn,
As the sun rises and the sky turns blue,
Makes me think, for you is why I was born,
And so to, I know I'm in love with you.

A woman of fine tuned intent unleashed,
So her love leaves me unable to speak,
But in the best way, my love is released,
And forms in ways that sits, ever unique.

You must be real to me, my soul knows yours,
And your love marks my heart with a deep scar,
Your love for me grows each day you assure,
I know the truest form of who you are.

In my dreams we are always together,
And in my heart you are safe forever.

Sonnet 52: rue

For the last time we meet now face to face,
Words would fail the emotions felt by us,
A long lasting although a final embrace,
Is all that can withstand this precipice.

Though I say for now, my heart is broken,
Careless was your actions, they pain me still,
This hurt now keeps me at night awoken,
As I sit alone on the window sill.

I think on the words you said to me last,
When you said the love you had is now gone,
I cling without hope to relive the past,
I would give it all up just to hold on.

Now for your actions you should solely rue,
And yet to this day I do still love you.

Sonnet 53: the words of my sonnet

Spirit lack and my soul is burnt out too,
But my heart hurts the most from this parting,
Alas I say as I am without you,
And so to I feel the sorrow starting.

I am now a house with no pictures hung,
My body is broken beyond repair,
Blackened skin that wraps up my paper lungs,
And eyes of black holes with a vacant stare.

But you live in the words of my sonnet,
Once we are all forgotten, you remain,
It is the job set out for the poet,
To bring you alive time and time again.

You always brought out the best side of me,
And always still, my heart belongs to thee.

Sonnet 54: the realisation

Where go you my love as you walk on by,
I now know you and I were not to last,
And yet we tried and we tried and we tried,
But our love has been gone now for years past.

You make me feel like I've never been born,
And I know that was wholly ignored too,
I don't know what I will do once you're gone,
And I know not what will become of you.

I was once hurt by your venomous bite,
And blind at first was I by your pink hue,
Judas did only what she thought was right,
And you know that song was not about you.

You are filled by hate, and it leaves you blind.
I know my face is still etched in your mind.

Sonnet 55: nightmare

Your dreams are fraught with nightmarish demons,
Chasing you till you wake in fear only,
You wake with thoughts of monsters and heathens,
But they are put to rest by me mostly.

Muffled words here and there provide insight,
Something that I can only imagine,
Yet the pain crushes when you sleep at night,
And I can't think of why this would happen.

Fear nothing now as I block out the noise,
And I'll sooth you when we are together,
I say onto you, can you hear my voice,
Cry no more as we are with each other.

As I wonder what these nightmares are for,
I bid thee calm and sweet sleep ever more.

Sonnet 56: brighter than the sun

I'm eclipsed when the sun shines on your face,
Your soul always glows but never this bright,
It's rays dance over you, filling your space,
And here it comes burning your skin just right.

To see the sun set, it would be too soon,
It is like a never ending goodbye,
But your smile glazed in sunlight, fills the room,
And for us all, your laugh calms brooding skies.

You are precious to us and shall remain,
To light up our hearts still when you are gone,
It shall bring us nothing but pouring rain,
Someday when we will all have to go on.

But for you the sky shall never go black,
The sun will smile at you and you'll smile back.

Sonnet 57: the guilty reflection

Some do say life has no meaning for us,
It comes in just to ruin your day dream,
Dreams are not real life so we must adjust,
To the truth of the world by any means.

And so now I ponder what is in store,
Though I am troubled by the regret felt,
As dying is a day worth living for,
But dirty were the cards that had been dealt.

I lie easily but soon I will crash,
Comprehend the words once spoken before,
And then I'll be, dancing on broken glass,
And throwing my life away evermore.

Alone at last in a cast iron state,
I sit here awaiting my written fate.

Sonnet 58: the prophet

You see people talk without listening,
The powerful praying on the weaker,
On the people who hear without speaking,
Making the weak fall down even deeper.

Still their prophetic words flow through the air,
Then are caught and engraved in subway walls,
For everyone to see, the words are there,
For everyone to know and share for all.

And so the weaker willed people go on,
Trudging through the world with no help to them,
Until the feeling of regret is gone,
But then it always comes back once again.

Still moving on until they cannot bare,
Just wanting to be heard, but who will care.

Sonnet 59: I do

Take this hand, as I am on bended knee,
Take this ring, and hear the words that I say,
Take me in your arms, sing softly to me,
Take my heart, with all my love, on this day.

Listen now before we run out of time,
My dreams were made to be built around you,
I am yours for as long as you are mine,
Say it once, then I'll know our love is true.

Sit with me now and have this life with me,
For the moment the world is still out there,
You lull me to sleep as you sing softly,
Three words and you show me how much you care.

I am a heart that loved, but at what cost,
A heart that leads with love, is never lost.

Yes.